A catalogue of British insects. By John Reinhold Forster, ...

Johann Reinhold Forster

ECCO
PRINT EDITIONS

Gale ECCO Print Editions

Relive history with *Eighteenth Century Collections Online*, now available in print for the independent historian and collector. This series includes the most significant English-language and foreign-language works printed in Great Britain during the eighteenth century, and is organized in seven different subject areas including literature and language; medicine, science, and technology; and religion and philosophy. The collection also includes thousands of important works from the Americas.

The eighteenth century has been called "The Age of Enlightenment." It was a period of rapid advance in print culture and publishing, in world exploration, and in the rapid growth of science and technology – all of which had a profound impact on the political and cultural landscape. At the end of the century the American Revolution, French Revolution and Industrial Revolution, perhaps three of the most significant events in modern history, set in motion developments that eventually dominated world political, economic, and social life.

In a groundbreaking effort, Gale initiated a revolution of its own: digitization of epic proportions to preserve these invaluable works in the largest online archive of its kind. Contributions from major world libraries constitute over 175,000 original printed works. Scanned images of the actual pages, rather than transcriptions, recreate the works *as they first appeared.*

Now for the first time, these high-quality digital scans of original works are available via print-on-demand, making them readily accessible to libraries, students, independent scholars, and readers of all ages.

For our initial release we have created seven robust collections to form one the world's most comprehensive catalogs of 18th century works.

Initial Gale ECCO Print Editions collections include:

History and Geography
Rich in titles on English life and social history, this collection spans the world as it was known to eighteenth-century historians and explorers. Titles include a wealth of travel accounts and diaries, histories of nations from throughout the world, and maps and charts of a world that was still being discovered. Students of the War of American Independence will find fascinating accounts from the British side of conflict.

Social Science

Delve into what it was like to live during the eighteenth century by reading the first-hand accounts of everyday people, including city dwellers and farmers, businessmen and bankers, artisans and merchants, artists and their patrons, politicians and their constituents. Original texts make the American, French, and Industrial revolutions vividly contemporary.

Medicine, Science and Technology

Medical theory and practice of the 1700s developed rapidly, as is evidenced by the extensive collection, which includes descriptions of diseases, their conditions, and treatments. Books on science and technology, agriculture, military technology, natural philosophy, even cookbooks, are all contained here.

Literature and Language

Western literary study flows out of eighteenth-century works by Alexander Pope, Daniel Defoe, Henry Fielding, Frances Burney, Denis Diderot, Johann Gottfried Herder, Johann Wolfgang von Goethe, and others. Experience the birth of the modern novel, or compare the development of language using dictionaries and grammar discourses.

Religion and Philosophy

The Age of Enlightenment profoundly enriched religious and philosophical understanding and continues to influence present-day thinking. Works collected here include masterpieces by David Hume, Immanuel Kant, and Jean-Jacques Rousseau, as well as religious sermons and moral debates on the issues of the day, such as the slave trade. The Age of Reason saw conflict between Protestantism and Catholicism transformed into one between faith and logic -- a debate that continues in the twenty-first century.

Law and Reference

This collection reveals the history of English common law and Empire law in a vastly changing world of British expansion. Dominating the legal field is the *Commentaries of the Law of England* by Sir William Blackstone, which first appeared in 1765. Reference works such as almanacs and catalogues continue to educate us by revealing the day-to-day workings of society.

Fine Arts

The eighteenth-century fascination with Greek and Roman antiquity followed the systematic excavation of the ruins at Pompeii and Herculaneum in southern Italy; and after 1750 a neoclassical style dominated all artistic fields. The titles here trace developments in mostly English-language works on painting, sculpture, architecture, music, theater, and other disciplines. Instructional works on musical instruments, catalogs of art objects, comic operas, and more are also included.

The BiblioLife Network

This project was made possible in part by the BiblioLife Network (BLN), a project aimed at addressing some of the huge challenges facing book preservationists around the world. The BLN includes libraries, library networks, archives, subject matter experts, online communities and library service providers. We believe every book ever published should be available as a high-quality print reproduction; printed on-demand anywhere in the world. This insures the ongoing accessibility of the content and helps generate sustainable revenue for the libraries and organizations that work to preserve these important materials.

The following book is in the "public domain" and represents an authentic reproduction of the text as printed by the original publisher. While we have attempted to accurately maintain the integrity of the original work, there are sometimes problems with the original work or the micro-film from which the books were digitized. This can result in minor errors in reproduction. Possible imperfections include missing and blurred pages, poor pictures, markings and other reproduction issues beyond our control. Because this work is culturally important, we have made it available as part of our commitment to protecting, preserving, and promoting the world's literature.

GUIDE TO FOLD-OUTS MAPS and OVERSIZED IMAGES

The book you are reading was digitized from microfilm captured over the past thirty to forty years. Years after the creation of the original microfilm, the book was converted to digital files and made available in an online database.

In an online database, page images do not need to conform to the size restrictions found in a printed book. When converting these images back into a printed bound book, the page sizes are standardized in ways that maintain the detail of the original. For large images, such as fold-out maps, the original page image is split into two or more pages

Guidelines used to determine how to split the page image follows:

• Some images are split vertically; large images require vertical and horizontal splits.
• For horizontal splits, the content is split left to right.
• For vertical splits, the content is split from top to bottom.
• For both vertical and horizontal splits, the image is processed from top left to bottom right.

A
CATALOGUE
OF
BRITISH
INSECTS.

By JOHN REINHOLD FORSTER, F.A.S.

WARRINGTON.

Printed by WILLIAM EYRES.

MDCCLXX.

THE author of this catalogue intends to publish a *Fauna* of *British Insects*; and as he thinks not to set out upon it, till he can offer to the public a work, as little imperfect as possible, and to give no other descriptions than from ocular inspection he presents his most respectful compliments to all ladies and gentlemen who collect insects, and begs them to favour him, if possible, with specimens of such insects, as they can spare, and which he is not possessed of for this purpose he has made this catalogue, and put no mark to the insects in his possession, those which he has so plentifully as to be enabled to give some of them to other collectors, are marked with a (*d*); those which he has not, are marked either *Berk* signifying *Dr Berkenhout's Outlines of the Natural History of Great Britain*, or *B* signifying a manuscript catalogue of *British Insects* communicated to the author, or *B B* which signifies *Berkenhout*, together with the manuscript catalogue *N S* is put to such insects as have not yet been described by Dr *Linnæus*, and are *new species* with new specific names If therefore the author should be so happy as to be favoured with specimens, he will acknowledge the favour publickly, and give in return to any collector who desires to exchange, such insects as he can spare This catalogue contains 1000 insects, the *Swedes* have near 1700, it would therefore be an honour to this country, to scrutinize carefully into the various branches of *Natural History*, and to give the public as perfect and extensive catalogues of *British Animals* as possible The four first classes, containing *Quadrupeds, Birds, Reptiles* and *Fish*, have been so well and perfectly described by *Thomas Pennant* Esq, that it would be a disparagement, if the insects should be described defectively Put as Mr *Pennant* has given up this branch to the author, he will do his utmost to give his work all the perfection which lies in his power. Therefore he takes this opportunity to shew the ladies and gentlemen collectors, how far he is gone by three years assiduous collecting in the neighbourhood of *Warrington*, and to enable at the same time the spirited and patriotic promotors of knowledge, and especially of Natural History in *Great Britain*, to contribute towards perfecting the Natural History of their own country

DRAWINGS and scientific descriptions of such insects as are not yet described by *Linnæus* will be still more acceptable, and engage the publisher's thanks and acknowledgments

Jos: Banks

WARRINGTON,
August the 1st.
1770.

A

CATALOGUE

OF

BRITISH INSECTS.

I. COLEOPTERA.

1 SCARABÆUS.

1 1	Typhœus	
2 2	Lunaris. B. B.	
3 3	Cylindricus.	d.
4 4	Nuchicornis.	
5 5	Vacca B	
6 6	Erraticus. B.	
7 7	Foffor	
8 8	Fimetarius.	d
9 9	Hæmorrhoidalis. B.	
10 10	Confpurcatus	
11 11	Stercorarius	d
12 12	Vernalis Berkenh.	
13 13	Ovatus B	
14 14	Sabulofus.	
15 15	Fullo B	
16 16	Horticola.	d
17 17	Melolontha.	d.
18 18	Solftitialis. B. B.	
19 19	Occidentalis. B	
20 20	Hemipterus. Berkenh.	
21 21	Brunnus.	
22 22	Auratus. B. B.	
23 23	Quifquilius.	

24 24 Nobilis. Berkenh.
25 25 Rufipes

2. LUCANUS.

26 1 Cervus B B
27 2 Parallelepipedus.
28 3 Caraboides Berkenh.

3 DERMESTES.

29 1	Lardarius.	
30 2	Undatus. B.	
31 3	Pellio.	
32 4	Violaceus. B.	
33 5	Feneftralis.	
34 6	Melanocephalus. B.	
35 7	Domefticus Berkenh.	
36 8	Scarabæoides.	d
37 9	Murinus B	
38 10	Fumatus	
39 11	Pulicarius Berkenh	
40 12	Pfyllius B	
41 13	Scanicus. B.	
42 14	Colon	

A 2

4 HISTER.

4. HISTER.

43 1 Unicolor.   d.
44 2 Pygmæus.
45 3 Bimaculatus.
46 4 Striatus. N S.

5. CISTELA,

A Genus not in *Linnæus*, and only taken from *Geoffroy*
47 1 *Fasciata.* N S. Geoff 1. d.
48 2 *Pustulata* N S Geoff 2.
49 3 *Nigra.* N S. Geoff 3.
50 4 *Striata.* N S
51 5 *Sericea* N S.   d

6. BYRRHUS.

52 1 Scrophulariæ. Berk.
53 2 Verbasci.

7. GYRINUS.

54 1 Natator.   d

8. SILPHA.

55 1 Germanica.
56 2 Vespillo.   d.
57 3 Bipustulata. B. B.
58 4 4-Pustulata. B. B.
59 5 Littoralis.
60 6 Atrata
61 7 Thoracica.   a
62 8 4-Punctata.   d.
63 9 Opaca.
64 10 Rugosa.
65 11 Sabulosa B. B
66 12 Obscura.   d
67 13 Rufipes
68 14 Aquatica.   d.
69 15 Colon B.   &
70 16 Grisea. B
71 17 Pulicaria. Berkenh.
72 18 Pedicularia. B.

9 CASSIDA.

73 1 Viridis.

74 2 Murræa. *B.*
75 3 Nebulosa *B B*
76 4 Nobilis *B. B*
77 5 Maculata. *B. B.*
78 6 *Pallida.* N S.

10 CURCULIO.

79 1 Alliariæ.
80 2 Cyaneus. *B. B.*
81 3 Badensis.
82 4 Aterrimus.
83 5 Cerasi.
84 6 Pruni. Berkenh.
85 7 Acridulus *B. B.*
86 8 Purpureus. B. B.
87 9 Frumentarius.
88 10 Granarius. Berkenh.
89 11 Dorsalis. Berkenh.
90 12 Pini. Berkenh.
91 13 Lapathi.
92 14 Scaber.
93 15 Quercus Berkenh
94 16 Viscariæ. Berkenh.
95 17 *Ulicis.* N S.
96 18 5-Maculatus. *B. B.*
97 19 Pericarpius. Berk.
98 20 Anguinus.
99 21 Bacchus
100 22 Betulæ
101 23 Populi
102 24 Alni *B B*
103 25 *Rufulus* N S.
104 26 Salicis
105 27 Fagi B B
106 28 Beccabungæ Berk
107 29 Obscurus. N S.
108 30 Pemorum.
109 31 Germanus B.
110 32 Nucum B B.
111 33 Rumicis.
112 34 Scrophulariæ.   d.
113 35 *Similis* N S.   d.
114 36 *Dissimilis.* N S.   d.
115 37 4-*Guttatus.* N S   d.

116

116 38 *Pollinarius.* N S.
117 39 *Longimanus.* N S.
118 40 Druparum.
119 41 Violaceus. B.
120 42 Tortrix. Berk.
121 43 Lineatus.
122 44 Incanus.
123 45 *Melanogrammus.* N S
124 46 Nebulofus. Berkenh.
125 47 Exfoletus. N S   *d.*
126 48 Liguftici.
127 49 Ovatus.
128 50 Cervinus
129 51 Oblongus.
130 52 Pyri
131 53 Argentatus.

11 ATTELABUS

132 1 Coryli. Berkenh.
133 2 Avellanæ.   *d*
134 3 Curculionoides.
135 4 Betulæ.   *d.*

12 CLERUS

Of *Geoffroy*; with *Linnæus* they
are fpecies of *Attelabi*

136 1 Apiarius   *B B*
137 2 Formicarius   *B B.*
138 3 Mollis. *B*
139 4 *Pilofus.* N S
140 5 *Cylindricus.* N S

13. ANTHRIBUS,

A genus not in *Linnæus*, and in
Geoffroy only

141 1 *Fafciatus.* N S. Geoff 1.
142 2 *Nebulofus.* N S. Geoff. 2.

14. COCCINELLA.

143 1 Unipunctata *B.*
144 2 Bipunctata.   *d*
145 3 5-Punctata *B B*
146 4 6-Punctata. *B.*
147 5 7-Punctata.   *d.*

148 6 9-Punctata.
149 7 11-Punctata.
150 8 12-Punctata. B.
151 9 13-Punctata.
152 10 13-*Maculata* N S.   *d.*
153 11 14-Punctata.
154 12 16-Punctata Berk.
155 13 19-Punctata.   *d.*
156 14 22-Punctata
157 15 25-Punctata.
158 16 Conglobata. Berkenh.
159 17 14-Guttata.   *d.*
160 18 2 Puftulata.
161 19 4-Puftulata.   *d.*
162 20 6-Puftulata.
163 21 10-Puftulata.   *d.*
164 22 Pantherina B.

15 PTINUS.

165 1 Pectinicornis B B.
166 2 Pertinax. Berk.
167 3 Mollis. Berk.
168 4 Imperialis. B.
169 5 Fur.   *d*

16. BRUCHUS.

170 1 Granarius B

17 CHRYSOMELA.

171 1 Tanaceti.
172 2 Hæmorrhoidalis B
173 3 Graminis. B B.
174 4 Ænea. B.
175 5 Alni   *d*
176 6 Betulæ   *d.*
177 7 Hæmoptera.
178 8 Cerafi.
179 9 Padi.
180 10 Armoraciæ B.
181 11 Cerealis Berkenh.
182 12 Faftuofa
183 13 Vitellinæ   *d.*
184 14 Polygoni. B. B.
185 15 Pallida.

186 16 Staphylea.	d	228 5 Flava.
187 17 Polita. '	d	229 6 *Teſtacea* N S.
188 18 *Hyperici* N S.	d.	230 7 *Melanopa.* N S.
189 19 Populi.		231 8 *Faſciata.* N S.
190 20 10-Punĉtata. *B*		232 9 *Clavicornis* N S.
191 21 Boleti *B*		
192 22 Sanguinolenta. *B. B.*		**19 CANTHARIS**
193 23 *Olivacea.* N S.	d.	*(Meloe* of *Linnæus.)*
194 24 Marginata.	d.	233 1 Proſcarabæus
195 25 Marginella.	d	234 2 Veſicatoria. *B.*
196 26 4-Punĉtata. *B B.*		235 3 Floralis. *B.*
197 27 2-Punĉtata Berk.		
198 28 Sericea.	d.	**20 TENEBRIO**
199 29 Merdigera. *B.*		236 1 Molitor. *B B.*
200 30 *Cratægi.* N S.		237 2 Culinaris.
201 31 Caprææ		238 3 Foſſor.
202 32 Nymphææ.	d.	239 4 Pallens.
203 33 Cyanella.		240 5 Mortiſagus. *B B.*
204 34 Melanopa.		241 6 Cæruleus.
205 35 Flavipes		242 7 *Violaceus* N S.
206 36 12-Punĉtata. Berk.		243 8 Roſtratus
207 37 Phellandrii *B B*		
208 38 Aſparagi. *B B*		**21 DYTISCUS.**
209 39 Ceramboides. *B*		244 1 Latiſſimus Berk.
210 40 Hirta.		245 2 Marginalis.
211 41 Elongata *B.*		246 3 Semiſtriatus.
212 42 Oleracea.		247 4 Striatus
213 43 Chryſocephala.		248 5 Cinereus.
214 44 Hyoſcyami		249 6 Sulcatus.
215 45 Atricilla.		250 7 Maculatus.
216 46 Erythrocephala.		251 8 Bipuſtulatus.
217 47 Helxines.		252 9 Uliginoſus.
218 48 Exſoleta.		253 10 Granularis
219 49 Nitidula.	d	254 11 Minutus *B.*
220 50 Nemorum.		255 12 Piceus *B B.*
221 51 Fuſcicornis. *B.*		256 13 Caraboides. *B B.*
222 52 *Xanthogona.* N S.		257 14 Scarabæoides. *B.*
223 53 *Thoracica* N S.		258 15 Fuſcipes, Berkenh.

18. MORDELLA.

22. CARABUS.

224 1 Aculeata. *B B.*	259 1 Coriaceus.
225 2 Humeralis.	260 2 Granulatus.
226 3 Frontalis.	261 3 Hortenſis.
227 4 Thoracica.	

262 4 Leucophthalmus
263 5 Clatratus.
264 6 Violaceus. B B.
265 7 Sycophanta. B
266 8 Crepitans. B B.
267 9 Cyanocephalus
268 10 Melanocephalus
269 11 Ferrugineus.
270 12 Germanus
271 13 Vulgaris.
272 14 Cupreus.
273 15 Piceus.
274 16 Velox
275 17 Cærulefcens
276 18 Uftulatus
277 19 Crux minor
278 20 Sexpunctatus. Berk.

23 CICINDELA

279 1 Campeftris
280 2 Hybrida. *B.*
281 3 Riparia
282 4 Flavipes.
283 5 Aquatica.

24 BUPRESTIS

284 1 Chryfoftigma. Berk
285 2 Ruftica
286 3 Minuta *B*
287 4 Viridis *B*
288 5 Granularis Berk.
289 6 *Fuliginofa.* N S.

25 ELATER

290 1 Bipuftulatus.
291 2 Brunneus.
292 3 Ruficollis Berk
293 4 Mefomelus.
294 5 Caftaneus.
295 6 Livens. *B.*
296 7 Sangiuneus. Berk.
297 8 Balteatus. *B* B.
298 9 Sputator. *B.*
299 10 Obfcurus.
300 11 Murinus.

301 12 Teffelatus
302 13 Æneus
303 14 Pectinicornis.
304 15 Niger.
305 16 Linearis.

26 LAMPYRIS.

306 1 Noctiluca.
N B. The author has not got
the males of this fpecies
307 2 Coccinea   *d*

27. MALACOPTERYX.
(*Cantharis* of *Linnæus*)

308 1 Fufcus.   *d.*
309 2 Lividus.   *d.*
310 3 Obfcurus   *d*   *l*
311 4 Æneus   *d*
312 5 Bipuftulatus.   *d.*
313 6 Rufus
314 7 Fafciatus. Berkenh.
315 8 Biguttatus Berkenh.
316 9 Minimus.
317 10 Teftaceus *B*
318 11 Cæruleus *B.*
319 12 Melanurus.   *d.*
320 13 Navalis.

28. LEPTURA.

321 1 Aquatica.   *d.*
322 2 Melanura.   *d.*
323 3 Rubra
324 4 Teftacea
325 5 Virens. Berkenh.
326 6 Sexmaculata. *B.*
327 7 4-Fafciata *B.*
328 8 Attenuata   *d*
329 9 Myftica.
330 10 Arcuata. *B.*
331 11 Præufta. *B. B.*
332 12 Arietis.   *d.*

29. CERAMBYX.

333 1 Coriarius *B B*

334 2 Nebulofus.
335 3 Hifpidus.
336 4 Mofchatus.
337 5 Ædilis B.
338 6 Lamed B.
339 7 Inquifitor.
340 8 Fuliginator.
341 9 Scalaris.
342 10 Populneus. B
343 11 Rufticus Berkenh.
344 12 Violaceus B
345 13 Bajulus. B
346 14 Sanguineus. Berk.

30. STAPHYLINUS
347 1 Murinus.

348 2 Erythropterus.
349 3 Maxillofus.
250 4 Politus.
351 5 Rufus. Berkenh.
352 6 Riparius Berkenh.
d 353 7 Chryfomelinus Berk.
d. 354 8 Fufcipes
355 9 Rufipes.

31 NECYDALIS.
356 1 Cærulea.
357 2 Cerambordes. N S.

32. FORFICULA.
358 1 Auricularia B. B.
359 2 Minor.

II. HEMIPTERA.

I BLATTA
360 1 Orientalis. Berk.
361 2 Germanica.

2. GRYLLUS.
362 1 Bipunctatus Berk
363 2 Subulatus
364 3 Gryllotalpa Berk.
365 4 Domefticus
366 5 Campeftris Berk
367 6 Verrucivorus. Berk.
368 7 Groffus

3 CICADA
369 1 Cornuta.   d.
370 2 Spumaria.   d.
371 3 Nervofa
372 4 Albifrons.
373 5 Leucocephala. Berk.
374 6 Lateralis. Berk.

375 7 Striata B. B
376 8 Lineata
377 9 Interrupta.
378 10 Lanio.
379 11 Marginata
380 12 Viridis
381 13 Flava
382 14 Aurata
383 15 Ulmi Berkenh
384 16 Rofæ Berkenh

4. NOTONECTA.
385 1 Glauca   d.
386 2 Striata   d.
387 3 Minutiffima. Berk.

5. NEPA.
388 1 Cinerea.
389 2 Cimicoides.
390 3 Linearis.

6. CIMEX.

6. CIMEX.

391 1 Lectularius.
392 2 Scarabæoides Berk.
393 3 Clavicornis. Berk.
394 4 Corticalis Berk.
395 5 Betulæ Berk
396 6 Filicis. Berkenh
397 7 Rufipes.   d.
398 8 Marginatus. Berkenh.
399 9 Griseus.
400 10 Baccarum. Berkenh.
401 11 Juniperinus Berk
402 12 Prasinus
403 13 Cæruleus. Berkenh
404 14 Oleraceus. Berkenh.
405 15 Bicolor Berkenh
406 16 Acuminatus Berk.
407 17 Personatus Berk.
408 18 Ater.
409 19 Hyoscyami. Berk.
410 20 Equestris. Berkenh.
411 21 Apterus. Berkenh.
412 22 Pabulinus
413 23 Pratensis Berkenh.
414 24 Campestris
415 25 Umbratilis. Berk.
416 26 Nemorum.
417 27 Dolabratus.
418 28 Striatus Berkenh.
419 29 Populi
420 30 Ulmi. Berkenh.
421 31 Sylvestris
422 32 Abietis. Berkenh.
423 33 Lacustris
424 34 Stagnorum
425 35 Vagabundus Berk.

7 APHIS.

426 1 Ribis.   ⎫
427 2 Ulmi   ⎬ Berkenh.
428 3 Sambuci. ⎭

429 4 Rumicis.   ⎫
430 5 Acetosæ.   ⎪
431 6 Lychnidis.   ⎪
432 7 Rosæ.   ⎪
433 8 Tiliæ.   ⎪
434 9 Brassicæ.   ⎪
435 10 Craccæ.   ⎪
436 11 Sonchi   ⎪
437 12 Cardui.   ⎪
438 13 Tanaceti.   ⎬ Berkenh.
439 14 Absinthii.   ⎪
440 15 Jaceæ.   ⎪
441 16 Betulæ.   ⎪
442 17 Fagi.   ⎪
443 18 Quercus.   ⎪
444 19 Salicis.   ⎪
445 20 Populi.   ⎪
446 21 Aceris   ⎪
447 22 Atriplicis   ⎭

8 CHERMES.

448 1 Graminis.   ⎫
449 2 Pyri   ⎪
450 3 Sorbi.   ⎪
451 4 Urticæ.   ⎬ Berkenh.
452 5 Alni   ⎪
453 6 Quercus   ⎪
454 7 Abietis.   ⎪
455 8 Fraxini.   ⎭

9 COCCUS.

456 1 Hesperidum ⎫
457 2 Phalaridis. ⎬ Berkenh.
458 3 Betulæ.   ⎭

10 THRIPS.

459 1 Minutissima.   ⎫
460 2 Physapus   ⎪
461 3 Juniperina   ⎬ Berkenh.
462 4 Fasciata.   ⎭

B

III.

III. LEPIDOPTERA.

1 PAPILIO.

463	1	Machaon } Berk	
464	2	Podalirius. }	
465	3	Cratægi	
466	4	Brassicæ.	d.
467	5	Rapæ	d
468	6	Napi	d
469	7	Sinapis	
470	8	Cardamines.	d.
471	9	Hyale. Berkenh.	
472	10	Rhamni.	d.
473	11	Hyperantus.	d
474	12	Io	d
475	13	Mæra,	d
476	14	Mægæra.	d.
477	15	Ægeria.	d
478	16	Galathea.	
479	17	Semele.	
480	18	Jurtina	d
481	19	Janira.	d.
482	20	Cardui. B. B	
483	21	Iris B. B	
484	22	Antiopa B B.	
485	23	Polychloros	
486	24	Urticæ	d.
487	25	C. Album.	
488	26	Atalanta	
489	27	Lucina Berkenh	
490	28	Maturna	d
491	29	Cinxia Berkenh	
492	30	Paphia.	d.
493	31	Aglaia.	d
494	32	Adippe.	
495	33	Lathonia. Berkenh	
496	34	Euphrosyne.	d
497	35	Betulæ.	
498	36	Quercus.	
499	37	Argus.	
500	38	Argiolus.	
501	39	Rubi	
502	40	Pamphilus.	
503	41	Phlæas Berkenh.	
504	42	Virgaureæ.	d.
505	43	Comma.	d
506	44	Malvæ	
507	45	Tages	d

2 SPHINX.

508	1	Ocellata. Berkenh.	
509	2	Populi.	
510	3	Tiliæ B. B.	
511	4	Convolvuli. B. B.	
512	5	Ligustri. B. B	
513	6	Atropos B. B.	
514	7	Elpenor. B B	
515	8	Porcellus B B	
516	9	Stellatarum. B B	
517	10	Fuciformis	
518	11	Apiformis B	
519	12	Culiciformis B.	
520	13	Vespiformis B	
521	14	Tipuliformis.	
522	15	Filipendulæ	d,
523	16	Statices	

3 PHALÆNA

524	1	Pavonia. Berk.	
525	2	Quercifolia B B	
526	3	Rubi B B	
527	4	Potatoria B B	
528	5	Pini B B	
529	6	Quercus B B	
530	7	Lanestris. B. B.	
531	8	Vinula.	
532	9	Bucephala B. B	
533	10	Versicolora. B. B	
534	11	Populi Berkenh.	
535	12	Neustria Berkenh.	
536	13	Caja.	
537	14	Villica. B. B.	
538	15	Plantaginis	
539	16	Monacha B B	
540	17	Dispar. B. B.	

541	18	Chryforrhoea.	
542	19	Salicis. B B	
543	20	Coryli Berkenh.	
544	21	Pudibunda.	
545	22	Fafcelina.	
546	23	Antiqua.	
547	24	Gonoftigma B. B.	
548	25	Cæruleocephala. B. B.	
549	26	Ziczac. B B.	
550	27	Coffus B B	
551	28	Aulica? B.	
552	29	Lubricipeda.	
553	30	Ruffula. Berkenh.	
554	31	Libatrix.	
555	32	Oo B. B.	
556	33	Hnmuli	
557	34	Dominula. B. B.	
558	35	Fuliginofa.	
559	36	Glyphica	
560	37	Mi	
561	38	Jacobææ.	
562	39	Rubricollis	
563	40	Quadra B B.	
564	41	Complana.	
565	42	Nupta B B	
566	43	Pacta B B.	
567	44	Pronuba	
568	45	Maura	
569	46	Fraxini B B.	
570	47	Chryfitis.	
571	48	Gamma	
572	49	Interrogationis	
573	50	Jota?	
574	51	Feftucæ B B	
575	52	Meticulofa	
576	53	Pfi	
577	54	Chi	
578	55	Aceris B B	
579	56	Nictitans.	
580	57	Perficaria.	
581	58	Exfoleta B. B.	
582	59	Verbafci.	
583	60	Plecta.	
584	61	Derafa.	
585	62	Brafficæ.	
586	63	Rumicis.	

d.	587	64	Oxyacanthæ. B. B.	
	588	65	Polyodon.	
	589	66	Oleracea.	
	590	67	Pifi B. B.	
	591	68	Atriplicis. B. B.	
	592	69	Triplacia	
	593	70	Pyramidæa	
	594	71	Typica.	
	595	72	Delphinii B B	
	596	73	Citrago. B B.	
	597	74	Lactearia.	
d.	598	75	Putataria	
	599	76	Vibicaria.	
	600	77	Thymiaria	
	601	78	Punctaria	
	602	79	Amataria. B B.	
	603	80	Lacertinaria Berk.	
	604	81	Sambucaria	
d	605	82	Syringaria	
	606	83	Prunaria B B.	
d	607	84	Elinguaria	
d	608	85	Pulveraria	
	609	86	Betularia	
	610	87	Wavaria.	
	611	88	Pufaria	
	612	89	Papilionaria. B B	
d	613	90	Defoliaria Albin. t. 91. fig. G. H. I.	
	614	91	Viridata	
	615	92	Chærophyllata	d
d	616	93	Groffulariata	d.
	617	94	Cratægata.	d
	618	95	*Miniata* N S.	
	619	96	*Fulvata* N S.	
	620	97	Populata.	
	621	98	Bilineata	d.
	622	99	Chenopodiata.	
	623	100	Plagiata.	
	624	101	Prunata	
	625	102	Fluctuata	
	626	103	Remutata.	
	627	104	Alchemillata.	
	628	105	Marginata.	
	629	106	Urticata	
	630	107	Nymphæata.	
	631	108	Potamogata.	

632 109 Stratiotata.
633 110 Lemnata.
634 111 Brumata Berkenh.
635 112 Prasinana.
636 113 Viridana
637 114 Clorana. M B.
638 115 Hamana.
639 116 Oporana.
640 117 Bergmanniana.
641 118 Uddmanniana
642 119 Brunnichana
643 120 Proboscidalis
644 121 Rostralis. Berk.
645 122 Forficalis
646 123 Verticalis.
647 124 Pinguinalis
648 125 Evonymella.

649 126 Padella.
650 127 Culmella. Berk.
651 128 Salicella Berkenh.
652 129 Tapetzella. Berkenh.
653 130 Sarcitella. Berkenh.
654 131 Granella. Berkenh.
655 132 Serratella.
656 133 Pomonella B B.
657 134 Calthella
658 135 Swammerdamella.
659 136 Geoffrella
660 137 Frischella   d.
661 138 Rajella
662 139 Didactyla. Berkenh.
663 140 Pentadactyla Berk
664 141 Tridactyla
665 142 Hexadactyla.

IV. NEUROPTERA.

1 LIBELLULA.

666 1 4-Maculata.
667 2 Flaveola
668 3 Depressa
669 4 Vulgatissima Berk
670 5 Cancellata
671 6 Ænea.
672 7 Grandis Berkenh
673 8 Forcipata.
674 9 Virgo.
675 10 Puella.

2 RAPHIDIA

676 1 Ophiopsis B

3 EPHEMERA.

677 1 Vulgata.
678 2 Marginata
679 3 Vespertina Berk
680 4 Bioculata.
681 5 Fuscata. B.
682 6 Culiciformis. Berk.
683 7 Horaria Berk

684 8 Striata Berk
685 9 Diptera

4 PHRYGANEA

686 1 Bicaudata
687 2 Nebulosa. Berkenh.
688 3 Striata. Berkenh
689 4 Grisea B
690 5 Grandis. B.
691 6 Rhombica.
692 7 Flavilatera. Berk
693 8 Nigra Berk
694 9 Ciliaris.
695 10 Longicornis

5 HEMEROBIUS

696 1 Pectinicornis. Berkenh.
697 2 Perla.
698 3 Chrysops.
699 4 Albus
700 5 Hirtus.
701 6 Speciosus.
702 7 Sexpunctatus.

703 8 Humuli.

704 9 Lutarius.

6. PANORPA.

705 1 Communis.

7. MYRMELLON.

706 1 Formicarium. *Berk.*

V. HYMENOPTERA,

1. APIS.

707 1 Humulorum.

708 2 Centuncularis *Berk.*

709 3 Rufa

710 4 Bicornis

711 5 Florisomnis

712 6 Helvola.

713 7 Succincta.

714 8 Cærulescens.

715 9 Mellifica.

716 10 Cunicularia

717 11 Manicata *Berk*

718 12 4-Dentata

719 13 Conica

720 14 *Vernalis* N S

721 15 *Lamii.* N. S.

722 16 Ruficornis

723 17 Ferruginata.

724 18 Terrestris

725 19 Hortorum

726 20 Pratorum

727 21 Lapidaria.

728 22 Muscorum.

729 23 Acervorum

730 24 Subterranea *Berkenb*

731 25 *Pennipes* N S

2 FORMICA.

732 1 Herculeana.

733 2 Rufa

734 3 Nigra. } *Berkenh.*

735 4 Rubra

736 5 Fusca

3. VESPA.

737 1 Crabro

738 2 Vulgaris

739 3 Parietum.

740 4 Muraria.

741 5 Spinipes.

742 6 Coarctata. *Berkenh.*

4 CHRYSIS.

743 1 Ignita.

744 2 Aurata.

5 SIREX

745 1 Gigas. *Berkenh.*

746 2 Juvencus.

6 TENTHREDO.

747 1 Enodis

748 2 Ustulata.

749 3 *Cyanocrocea* N S.

750 4 *Atrata* N S.

751 5 Femorata. *Berkenb.*

752 6 Lutea *Berkenb*

753 7 Nitens.

754 8 *Arcuata.* N. S.

755 9 Rustica

756 10 Scrophulariæ

757 11 Abietis

758 12 Padi.

759 13 Salicis.

760 14 Atra.

761 15 Viridis.

762 16 Ovata.

763 17 Rosæ.

764 18 Bicincta.

765 19 Cincta.

766 20 Livida.

767 21 Nigra.

768

768 22 Naffata.
769 23 Cynofbati.
770 24 Caprææ.

7 CYNIPS

771 1 Glechomæ *Berkenh.*
772 2 Quercus baccarum.
773 3 Quercus folii.
774 4 Quercus petioli. *Berk.*
775 5 Quercus gemmæ. *Berk.*
776 6 Bedeguaris.
777 7 *Sericeus.* N S (Geoff 12)

8 SPHEX.

778 1 Sabulofa.   d.
779 2 Viatica   d.
780 3 Fufca   d
781 4 Cribraria.   d.
782 5 Fofforia   d
783 6 Leucoftoma
784 7 Pectinipes.
785 8 *Xanthocephala.* N S.
786 9 *Spinofa.* N S

9. ICHNEUMON

787 1 Luteus
788 2 Ramidulus
789 3 Luctatorius.
790 4 Perfuaforius. *Berkenh*

791 5 Fofforius.
792 6 Manifeftator.
793 7 Titillator
794 8 Inculcator *Berkenh*
795 9 Pugillator.
796 10 Rufpator. *Berkenh*
797 11 Corrufcator
798 12 Jaculator *Berkenh*
799 13 Prærogator.
800 14 *Primatorius.* N S.
801 15 *Xanthorius.* N S.
802 16 *Armatorius.* N S
803 17 *Polyzonias.* N S
804 18 Sugillatorius.
805 19 Sarcitorius.
806 20 Extenforius
807 21 Comitator *Berkenh*
808 22 Peregrinator *Berk*
809 23 Incubitor
810 24 *Atrator* N S
811 25 *Aterrimus* N S
812 26 Puparum *Berkenh*
813 27 Aphidum *Berkenh.*
814 28 Ovulorum.
815 29 Glomeratus.
816 30 Globatus. *Berkenh*
817 31 Pectinicornis. *Berk*

VI. DIPTERA.

1 TIPULA

818 1 Pectinicornis.
819 2 Rivofa.
820 3 Crocata.
821 4 Oleracea
822 5 Hortorum
823 6 Variegata.
824 7 Contaminata
825 8 Lunata. *Berkenh.*
826 9 Cornicina. *Berkenh.*
827 10 Atrata
828 11 Arundineti.
829 12 Plumofa. *Berkenh.*
830 13 Littoralis.
831 14 Motitatrix. *Berkenh*

832 15 Monilis *Berkenh.*
833 16 Thomæ
834 17 Johannis.
835 18 Brevicornis
836 19 Febrilis
837 20 Hortulana *Berk*
838 21 Phalænoides

2 CULEX.

839 1 Pipiens
840 2 Bifurcatus } *Berkenh.*
841 3 Pulcaris }

3 EMPIS.

842 1 Pennipes.
843 2 Livida
844 3 Stercorea.

4 ASILUS.

845 1 Crabroniformis *Berk*
846 2 Marginatus
847 3 Forcipatus
848 4 Oelandicus.
849 5 Tipuloides. *Berk.*
850 6 Morio.

5. CONOPS.

851 1 Rostratus
852 2 Calcitrans
853 3 Irritans
854 4 Vesicularis
855 5 Macrocephala *Berk*

6. BOMBYLIUS.

856 1 Major.
857 2 Medius.
858 3 Minor. *Berkenh.*

7. HIPPOBOSCA.

859 1 Equina } *Berkenh*
860 2 Hirundinis }

8. MUSCA.

861 1 Chamæleon.
862 2 Hydroleon *Berkenh*
863 3 Clavipes
864 4 *Vallata.* N S
865 5 *Chalybata* N S.
866 6 *Similis.* N S.
867 7 Morio. *Berkenh.*
868 8 Scolopacea.
869 9 Tringaria.
870 10 Bombylans.
871 11 Lappona.
872 12 *Pellita* N S (Sultzer's
     Tabanus Pellitus)
873 13 *Melanopyrrba.* N S.
874 14 Pendula.
875 15 Florea.
876 16 Arbustorum.
877 17 Nectarea.
878 18 Nemorum.
879 19 Intricaria.
880 20 Tenax.
881 21 Lucorum.
882 22 Sylvarum.
883 23 Bicincta.
884 24 Mutabilis.
885 25 Ichneumonea.
886 26 Arcuata

887 27 *Clavicornis.* N S.
888 28 Glaucia.
889 29 Noctiluca.
890 30 Ribesii.
891 31 Pyrastri.
892 32 Scripta
893 33 Mellina.
894 34 Menthastri.
895 35 Pipiens.
896 36 *Granditarsa.* N S.
897 37 Segnis.
898 38 Saltatrix.
899 39 Inanis. *Berkenh.*
900 40 Pellucens.
901 41 Meridiana
902 42 Cæsar.
903 43 Cadaverina.
904 44 Vomitoria.
905 45 Carnaria.
906 46 Domestica.
907 47 Maculata.
908 48 Fera.
909 49 Coemeteriorum
910 50 Cellaris *Berkenh*
911 51 Putris. *Berkenh.*
912 52 Polita.
913 53 Cupraria.
914 54 Nobilitata.
915 55 *Pennipes.* N S. (Scopoli)
916 56 Stercoraria.
917 57 Scybalaria.
918 58 Umbrarum.
919 59 Vibrans
920 60 Cynipsea.
921 61 Flava.
922 62 Germinationis
923 63 Heraclii.
924 64 Frondescentiæ.
925 65 Solstitialis.

9. TABANUS.

926 1 Bovinus.
927 2 Autumnalis.
928 3 Pluvialis.
929 4 Cæcutiens

10. OESTRUS.

930 1 Bovis
931 2 Hæmorrhoidalis. } *Berk.*
932 3 Ovis.

VII. AP-

VII. APTERA.

1. LEPISMA.
933 1 Saccharina. *Berk*
2. PODURA.
934 1 Viridis,
935 2 Plumbea,
936 3 Villofa,
937 4 Aquatica
Berk
3. TERMES.
938 1 Pulfatorium *Berk*
4 PEDICULUS.
939 1 Humanus.
940 2 Pubis,
941 3 Bovis,
942 4 Vituli,
943 5 Cervi,
944 6 Gallinæ,
945 7 Columbæ,
Berkenh
946 8 *Sturni*, N S.
5. PULEX.
947 1 Irritans
948 2 Penetrans? A.
6 ACARUS.
949 1 Reduvius. *Berkenh*
950 2 Ricinus
951 3 Pafferinus *Berkenh*
952 4 Telarius *Berkenh.*
953 5 Aquaticus.
954 6 Holofericeus
955 7 Coleoptratorum
956 8 Longicornis *Berkenh.*
7. PHALANGIUM.
957 1 Opilio *Berkenh.*
958 2 Cancroides.
959 3 Balænarum
8. ARANEA.
960 1 Diadema
961 2 Cucurbitina.
962 3 Domeftica.
963 4 Labyrinthica
964 5 Redimita
965 6 Montana.
966 7 Extenfa.
Berk.

967 8 Holofericea
968 9 Senoculata
969 10 Scenica
970 11 Aquatica
971 12 Viatica
Berk
10. CANCER.
972 1 Hexapus
973 2 Longicornis P
974 3 Mænas P.
975 4 Pagurus.
976 5 Bernhardus *Berkenh.*
977 6 Araneus *Berkenh*
978 7 Gammarus.
979 8 Aftacus. *B B*
980 9 Squilla
981 10 Crangon P
982 11 Norvegicus P.
983 12 Pulex *B B*
984 13 Locufta P
985 14 Linearis
986 15 Salinus *Berkenh.*
987 16 Stagnalis
11. MONOCULUS.
988 1 Pifcinus
989 2 Apus *Berkenh*
990 3 Pulex
991 4 Quadricornis.
⬤ 5 Conchaceus *Berk.*
12 ONISCUS.
993 1 Afilus
994 2 Entomon
Berk
995 3 Phyfodes.
996 4 Aquaticus *Berk.*
997 5 Afellus
998 6 Armadillo. *Berk.*
13. COLOPENDRA.
999 1 Lagura
1000 2 Forficata
1001 3 Electrica.
Berk.
1002 4 Marina
14. JULUS.
1003 1 Terreftris *Berk.*
1004 2 Sabulofus.

F I N I S.

Lightning Source UK Ltd.
Milton Keynes UK
UKOW021948100413

209030UK00004B/59/P

Old Cashmere Shawls: How They Are Made And Why The Art Is Lost...

Margaret Rives King

Old Cashmere Shawls.

How they are Made and why the
Art is Lost.

King, Margaret R.

———————————⬥———————————

Cincinnati:
Robert Clarke & Co., Printers,
1892.

A few years ago I was induced to put into print the result of some investigations I had made in the history and manufacture of " old Cashmere Shawls." The very small edition has been exhausted, and I have decided to make a second edition to meet the frequent demands for the little book by those who desire to study this beautiful art. It will be a handbook for the Cincinnati Museum, where can be found the best collection of rare " old Cashmere Shawls " certainly in this country, perhaps even the Museums of Europe can show nothing better. I am indebted for the information I have collected to Moorcroft, Vigne, Heeren, and Wakefield.

MARGARET R. KING.

CINCINNATI,
    OCTOBER, 1892.

Cashmere Shawls.

The most graceful and beautiful article of woman's wear is the shawl. Decorative and flowing, it is the most universally suitable garment that can adorn a woman's form. The shawl is of oriental origin, where it is worn alike by men and women. By far the most complete fabric comes from the looms and handicraft of Cashmere,* "the unequaled" as the Persians call that favored land, a little country of Asia, situated just north of the Punjab, among the Himalaya Mountains, 5,000 feet above the level of the sea, with Thibet adjoining on the east and Bokhara, the supposed cradle of civilization, on the north-west. Among the highlands and mountains of this beautiful region are found the sheep and goats which produce the fine wool used in the manufacture of these shawls.

The "*old Cashmere shawl*" was the treasure in the wardrobe of our grandmothers, and happy the woman whose careful ancestor had preserved one to come down through the years to her descendants in all its softness and delicacy of coloring. In this artistic age of correct taste such an admiration has grown up for the

* Kashmir is the oriental spelling of this word.

essentially

essentially beautiful, that the long negected old chests and closets have been ransacked and rummaged, and old shawls and old laces have been drawn forth from their lavender beds, once more to be admired and prized.

The general introduction of Cashmere shawls into Europe may be dated from the return of Napoleon Bonaparte from Egypt, where he had seen and admired and laid violent hands upon these beautiful garments so lavishly worn by the orientals. A furor sprung up among the women of the Empire, and no toilet was considered complete without the graceful folds of an oriental shawl.* Like all fashions this passed away, but, unlike the fate of the objects of frivolous taste, these beautiful fabrics were not destroyed nor bestowed upon the unappreciative, but carefully folded and put out of view, and from these stores are, without doubt, now drawn the exquisite textile wonders which have dropped upon us as if brought by a magician's wand.

Cincinnati is most especially fortunate, or rather the few elect among the women of Cincinnati are so, in finding themselves unexpectedly possessed of what before had been a dream or an image brought up after

* The Empress Josephine possessed over four hundred Cashmere shawls, and it is said (the authority being Mde. de Remusat) that one of the many weaknesses of the Emperor Napoleon was that he never wished to see the same shawl twice on the shoulders of his empress, and on more than one occasion in a rough manner tore the repeated shawl from her shoulders and dashed it in the fire.

reading the Arabian Nights, or some magical tale of the more hidden orient.

A beautiful taste, a generous heart, and an ample purse, united to form the power of the magician who was the source of all this happiness to Cincinnati women. We do not wish to lift the veil to see from whence and how these treasures came. It would be a romance which would tell the history of all the shawls which came to the generous benefactor who knew well where to place them and where their beauties would be best appreciated. The soft texture, the harmony of coloring, are salient points in these oriental works of art, but a deeper study will constantly develop new wonders of color and form.

To make the enjoyment of a Cashmere shawl perfect—how is it made? what are the different processes? and who are the people? are all questions which should be answered. Investigation has developed much to the writer, which is gladly dedicated to those fortunate ones who possess the inestimable treasure—

"An Old Cashmere Shawl."

But little mention is made of this beautiful vale of Cashmere in early historical records, but the traditions of the people make their importance and civilization of great antiquity. An early historical writer mentions a race in Northern India which certainly refers to the inhabitants of Cashmere—" people of fair complexion and beautiful in form and feature."

7   Reference

Reference is also made to the loom work of "splendid colors and brilliancy," which, without doubt, indicates those precious shawls, the most prized decoration, not only of the ladies of the West but much more so of the other sex in the East.

The shawl has a greater antiquity than any other garment. The most important manufacture of the Cashmere shawl was in the reign of Akbar, about the year 1556.

Heeren speaks of the "Happy Valley, as this fairy land is denominated throughout the East—the peaceful inhabitants sheltered for centuries from the revolution which devastated the rest of Asia. It is environed on all sides by a chain of mountains covered with perpetual snow, and can be approached only by two defiles on the bank of the Behud, which flows through its valley. · The soil seems to have been deposited by the stream, which at some distant period was arrested here and converted the whole valley into a lake, till it found at last an exit toward the South, in which direction the waters descend to join the Indus. The mud thus deposited, like that of the Nile, has become a soil which abundantly recompenses the husbandman. The height of the surrounding mountains defends the vale of Cashmere from the periodical rains which deluge the rest of India, and the lofty peaks are surmounted by the lighter and more feathery clouds which float in the upper regions of the atmosphere, and which descend in gentle

showers

showers, forming innumerable cascades, which precipitate themselves on all sides from the lofty and romantic walls of rock which encompass the valley and contribute to swell the stream by which it is divided. Protected by its peculiar position the fortunate valley suffers neither from the heat which prevails in the flats of Hindustan, nor feels the cold of the surrounding mountains. The fertile soil produces all the fruits known in temperate climes, and enjoys a perpetual spring, of which the nations of the North know nothing, except in the dreams of the poets."

For seven hundred years the Cashmerians have been followers of Mahomet, but evidences exist of a purer religion and higher civilization in the past. "Cashmere, although a part of India is not India. It has interests of a very different nature for the antiquarian, the architect, the geologist. Its monarchs have led their conquering armies to the subjugation of India, Ceylon, Thibet, and even to parts of China." A people must have had a past of culture to have reached the perfection of handicraft which still exists among them. Not only in the textile fabrics are they so skilled, and no nation has ever excelled the people of this valley in its beautiful shawls and carpets, but in carvings of wood and ivory, inlaid work in woods and mother of pearl, delicate painting, etc., they have always had and even now in their depressed condition still have a high degree of excellence. Advantages must have come to them from a civilized past, and

9   with

with this the advantage of environment has lent its aid. Never were people more blest in soil, climate, and productions—fruits and flowers of the highest excellence and beauty, the floating gardens, the lakes, covered with blooming water plants, the flat house-tops used as flower gardens. As the mountaineer descended from his home in the lofty fastnesses which entirely surround the vale of Cashmere, this beautiful sight met his eyes, and may have suggested the idea of that charming combination of color which is expressed in the " old shawls."

"The women of Cashmere to this day, notwithstanding hardships and privation, are a beautiful race, and are handsome enough to induce the exclamation, 'Who would despise a people that have among them such women?' Their beauty is what would be called the Jewish type, but rather might we say the Jews are of the Oriental type.

"The roses of Cashmere are even finer than the roses of Persia, and the rose water of Cashmere is far famed. A beautiful festival, the Feast of Roses, occurs about the first of May, when the plum trees and roses are in full bloom. The lotus, with its noble pink and white blossom, is very abundant and forms such a carpet over the lakes that the water hens walk freely about as if on dry ground without a fear of being immersed. Fountains abound and impart a delicious coolness to the air. The wild apricot trees, which bloom in the early spring, fill the air with

delicious

delicious fragrance, and the Cashmerian will come from afar to inhale it."

Such is the home of the old Cashmere shawl, and from these beautiful surroundings, and as the expression of a noble race, come to us these dreams of beauty.

The word shawl is derived from the native appellation of this graceful garment, *schal*. The wool which is used in the manufacture is of two kinds—the fleece of the domestic goat called *pasham schal* (or shawl wool) and that of the wild goat, wild sheep, and other animals, called *Asali Tus*.*

At one time the supply of wool was limited to the provinces of *Lesse* and *Ladikh*, but later large quantities were furnished by the great Kurghis Hords.

The preparation of the wool for the spinner is a very delicate operation. Much care is taken to separate the wool from the hair, for only the soft, delicate wool next the skin, which corresponds to the down of the eider-duck, is used for the fine shawls.

When the goat or sheep is sheared the long hair is first taken off, and is used for coarser fabrics and for making rope. The *pasham* for the shawl is taken

* The fine wool necessary for those soft and delicate shawls is a provision of nature to animals living in the highest regions, and the mountains around the vale of Cashmere seem to combine advantages over any other region for the production of this wool. Napoleon Bonaparte imported some of these goats into France, and a public spirited citizen of Essex county, England, also introduced them, but in both instances the wool deteriorated, and the goats were allowed to die out.

from

from the animal by combing, and is more readily disengaged by combing from the tail to the head.

Soap is never used in cleansing, as it is said to make the wool harsh and hard. In Hindustan, the shawl wool is washed with soap, which accounts for the fabrics of India failing to have the delicate softness of those of Cashmere. Husked rice is steeped in cold water until it becomes soft, when it is ground upon a stone slab to a fine consistence. It is then put between the layers of picked wool, which are squeezed with the hand until the wool is completely saturated with the mixture. After thus being treated, the wool is shaken and picked out and made into square pads called *Tumbu*. In this process the *Phiri* or second best wool is extracted, as only the finest is used for the best shawls. The *Phiri* is used for inferior shawls and for a coarse cloth, much used by the natives, called *Patu*. The *Tumbu* is then worked out in flat rolls, about half a yard long, and is folded up and deposited in a deep pot of red earthenware called *Taskas*, where it is left out of the way of dust or accident till required for the spinning-wheel. The wheel is constructed on the same principle as those used in Hindustan. It varies in finish. The rudest and cheapest is the *Takstidar*, the most serviceable the *Katsker*, and the best finished the *Pakhchedar*, used only by those who spin for amusement.

By an arrangement of the spindles and arms a soft elastic movement is produced, which insures evenness

12   and

and prevents the thread from breaking. The yarn is doubled and formed into twists the length required for the warp of a shawl.

Girls begin to spin at the age of ten, and one hundred thousand females were employed in the occupation in Cashmere. About one-tenth of the number were supposed to spin for the purpose of obtaining shawls for their own use and nine-tenths for their livelihood. After selecting the pattern the yarn is portioned according to the color and put in the hands of the dyer. If the body of the shawl is to be plain the finest wool is set aside for the center and the *Phiri* or seconds is sent to the dyers, the coarser being used for the figures and flowers, giving a raised appearance to the embroidery. The dyer prepares the yarn by steeping it in cold water and professes to give sixty-four tints. Each color has a special name; for instance, the scarlet is termed *Gulinar* (pomegranate flower). The best red is derived from cochineal, imported from Hindustan. Logwood is used for other red dyes. Blues and greens are dyed with indigo or coloring matter extracted from European broadcloths by boiling.

Carthemus and saffron grow in the provinces and furnish coloring for the various tints of orange, yellow, etc. The occupation of the dyer was invariably heriditary. The whiter and finer the wool of which the yarn is made, the more capable it is said to be of taking a brilliant color; for this reason the white wool

of

of the goat is preferred to that of the sheep—peculiar brilliancy is said to be imparted to color by the slanting rays of the setting sun. The *Nakatu* arranged the yarn for the warp and for the weft; that for the former is doubled and cut the proper lengths for a shawl. The number of these lengths vary from two thousand to three thousand, according to the closeness or openness of the texture, and the fineness or coarseness of the yarn. The weft is single and is estimated to weigh about half of the warp or woof. The *Nakatu* receives the yarn in hanks and returns it in balls. The warp is taken by the warp-dresser, is stretched, the thread being slightly separated, and is dressed by dipping it in boiled rice water. This process gives a certain stiffness or body. Silk is generally used for the warp on the border of a shawl. It has the advantage of showing the darker colors of the dyed wool more prominently than a warp of yarn, and moreover hardens and strengthens the border of the cloth. Where the border is narrow it is woven with the body of the shawl. When broad it is worked on a separate loom and sewed on the edge afterward by the *Rafugar* or fine-drawer with such nicety that it is difficult to detect the union. The operation of drawing the warp through the heddles is done in the same way as in Europe. The weavers were all males, commencing to learn at ten years, the same age at which the girls begin to learn to spin.

Shawls

Shawls are always made in pairs, and an ordinary pair will occupy three weavers for three months; a rich pair will occupy a shop for eighteen months. The loom does not differ in principle from the European loom. A *Usted* or master workman has from two to three hundred in a shop, and they are generally crowded together in long, low apartments.

When the warp is fixed in the loom, the pattern drawer and persons who determine the portion of yarn of different colors are again consulted. The first brings the drawing of the pattern in black and white. The *Taragaru*, having well considered it, points out the disposition of colors—beginning at the foot of the pattern and calling out the color and the number of threads to which it is to extend, that by which it is to be followed, and so on in succession till the whole pattern has been described.

From his dictation, the *Talimgaru* writes down the particulars in characters or short-hand and delivers a copy of the document to the weavers.

The workmen prepare the *tujis*, or needles, by arming each with colored yarn. These needles without eyes are made of light, smooth wood, slightly charred to prevent roughness from working. The face, or right side of the cloth, is placed next the ground— the work being carried on on the back or reverse, on which the needles hang in a row, numbering from four hundred to fifteen hundred, according to the lightness or heaviness of the embroidery. The cloth of shawls

generally

generally is of two kinds—one plain of two threads, one twilled or of four. The former was, in past times, wrought to a great degree of fineness, but later has been less in demand. Two persons have to be employed to weave the cloth shawl width. One throws the shuttle from the edge as far as he can across the warp, which is usually half way. It is then seized by the second weaver, who throws it on to the opposite side and returns it to his companion, who in turn forwards the shuttle. The cloth is often irregular, and when the texture is open it can be remedied by the introduction of additional threads—but there is no cure for that which is closer and more compacted. Occasionally pieces of cloth are found perfect in their regularity of texture. The higher the price, and the more elegant the border of the shawl, the more apt the structure of the cloth to be irregular. The edge of the warp is filled with the heavy thread of the *Phiri*, charged also with color, and to bring this into line the body of the cloth suffers. Foreign merchants are often so displeased with the irregularity of the field, that they cause the center to be removed and a new middle of even cloth to be inserted.

When the shawls are finished they are submitted to the *Purusgar*, or cleaner, whose business it is to free the shawl from discolored hairs or yarn, and from ends or knots, which they do with tweezers on the reverse side of the cloth. The purchaser takes the goods unwashed, and often in pieces, and the fine-drawer and

washer-woman

washer-woman have still their duty. The washing is done with clear, cold water, using soap very cautiously to white parts alone, and never to embroidery. Colored shawls are dried in the shade, white ones are bleached in the open air, and their color is improved by exposure to fumes of sulphur. After the shawls are washed they are stretched in a manner answering somewhat to calendering. A wooden cylinder in two parts is employed for this purpose, round which the shawl is folded and carefully wrapped, being occasionally damped to make it fold tighter. The end is sewed down, then two wedges are gradually driven between the two parts of the cylinder, at the open extremities, so as to force them asunder; then the shawl is stretched as tightly as its texture will admit. The shawl remains in this state for two days, when it is perfectly dry, and is unwrapped and put in a press before packing.

The worked shawl, or *Doschali Amri*, is worked entirely by needles with eyes, and with a particular kind of woolen thread. Woven shawls are made in separate pieces, and sewn together with such precision that the sewing is imperceptible. These are the most highly prized of the two.

Shawl manufacture is now the most important manufacture of the *Punjab*. Nearly a century ago, until which time it was almost entirely confined to Cashmere, a terrible famine occurred in this valley, and many of the shawl-weavers removed to the *Punjab*.

17   The

The best shawls of the *Punjab* are made at *Umritzur*, but none can compare with those of Cashmere—because the Punjab manufacturers are unable to obtain the finest wool; and, secondly, the inferiority in the dyeing, the excellence of which, in Cashmere, is attributed to some chemical peculiarity in the water. *Rampur* is a village in the *Sutlej* where the best wool is obtained, and the fabric made there is called the *Rampur Chudda.* A strict monopoly of best wool is kept in Cashmere.

The long shawl is called *Doschale.*

The square shawl, *Kussaba.*

The striped shawl, *Jamawars.*

White ground, with green sprigs, *Alfidar.*

Scarfs are worn about the waists by Asiatics, and are called *Schamlas.*

The center of the shawl is called *Mittan*, and when covered with work the shawl is called *Poor Mittan.*

The ornaments of the shawl are distinguished by different names—*Pala, Haschia, Zanghir, Dhour*, etc.

Pala, whole embroidery at both ends.

Haschia, border at each side of the whole length.

Zanghir, the chain which runs above and below the principal mass of the *Pala*, and as it were confines it.

Dhour, or running ornaments, is situated in the inside in regard to the *Haschia* and the *Zanghir*, enveloping immediately the whole field.

Kunjbutha, corner ornaments.

Butha is the generic term for flower, but is specifi-

18   cally

cally applied to the large cone-like ornaments which form the most prominent feature of the *Pala*. Each *Butha* consists of three parts—the *Pai*, or foot, usually a pediment of leaves, *Shikam*, or body, and *Sir*, or head. The head may be either erect or curved. The *Thal* is the net-work which separates the different *Buthas*.

The carpets made in Cashmere are woven in the same manner as the shawls, and are called *Khalin Pashminar*. Oriental names for colors: White, *Sada;* crimson, *Goolauer;* black, *Mooshkee;* purple, *Orda;* blue, *Ferozee;* green, *Zingaree;* yellow, *Zurd*.

There has never been a time when the offering of a Cashmere shawl was not considered the rarest and most beautiful gift that could be made to woman; and now more than ever to be valued must such a gift be, when we consider that this once beautiful and lovely region—the poet's own land—is now desolated by tyranny and famine, the result of a treaty made by the English at the close of the first Sikh war, in 1846, which gave over the beautiful vale of Cashmere to a soldier of fortune, the tyrant Gholab Singh.*

But, as early as the beginning of this century, the demand for Cashmere shawls was lessened by an

---

*It is an interesting fact to know that in Article X of the Amritzar treaty is the following: " Maharajah, Golab Singh acknowledges the supremacy of the British government, and will in token of such supremacy present annually to the British government one horse, twelve perfect shawl goats (six male and six female) and three pairs Kashmir shawls."

action of the Persian government putting a duty upon the importation of these articles of luxury, and discouraging their use in every way, that their own brocaded and embroidered shawl might come into more general use.

Many causes have combined to crush this handsome race. Their looms are hushed; their artists, dispirited, have abandoned work—and, perhaps, never more will be revived in its former perfection the beautiful art which was the expression of a joyous race, living a life of gladness in a land of plenty—the land of the rose and the jasmine—mingling their merry laughter with the music of the nightingale and the silver babbling of the clear waters which descended with joyous bounds from the surrounding mountains. Therefore, all ye fortunate ones who possess an old Cashmere shawl—cling to it, cherish it study its manifold beauties, and teach your children's children to reverence it.

20

Lightning Source UK Ltd.
Milton Keynes UK
UKOW021948100413

209030UK00004B/60/P